Copyright

MW00958987

Contents

WHAT IS A CONVECTION OVEN?

A convection oven has a powerful fan and exhaust system that circulates hot air inside the oven to help maintain a consistent temperature, making it ideal for multi-rack cooking. Like conventional ovens, convection ovens can be gas or electric and come in different models with various features.

One type of convection oven is a True convection oven. True convection, also called European convection or third-element convection, adds a third heating element in addition to the fan. With True convection, your dishes not only cook more evenly, but can even cook faster. Since True convection ovens have the potential to cook faster, they may require both time and temperature adjustments if you're using a recipe written for a conventional oven.

WHAT IS A CONVENTIONAL OVEN?

Conventional ovens, also called traditional, regular, thermal or radiant ovens, have heating elements that are typically located at the bottom and top of the oven. In a conventional oven, the dish closest to an active heating element cooks the fastest. In contrast, a convection fan circulates air throughout the cavity, reducing hot and cool spots that may cause dishes to cook faster or slower depending on their placement in the oven.

A conventional oven is what you might be most familiar with. Since most recipes are written for conventional ovens, people often feel more comfortable cooking with them because there's no need to adjust time or temperature to account for hot air circulation and faster cooking times1 like fan convection ovens sometimes require.

If you can't decide between convection and conventional, many ovens today are hybrid with both options built in. Most convection ovens have a convection setting that you can select as needed. Another option is a double oven with one thermal oven and one convection oven, so you can use one or both at the same time depending on what you're cooking or baking.

BENEFITS OF CONVECTION OVENS VS. CONVENTIONAL OVENS

Both convection and conventional ovens have benefits. See what each offers so you know what you want to bring home.

CONVECTION OVEN BENEFITS

- Circulating air helps dishes cook evenly

- Less rotating

- Improved browning and crisping

- Fast moving hot air accelerates baking and roasting1

- Quick preheating

- Easy to cook multiple dishes at once

- More flexibility to cook on multiple racks

- Recommended for cooking practically everything, including meats, vegetables, casseroles and cookies

With convection ovens, consistent heat helps meat get brown and crispy on the outside while staying juicy and tender on the inside.

CONVENTIONAL OVEN BENEFITS

- Most recipes are written for conventional ovens

- A more familiar cooking method

- Recommended for certain baked goods like delicate cakes and quick breads

Maytag offers both convection and conventional ovens. Browse our line of ranges and wall ovens to find the best fit for your home.

HOW TO USE A CONVECTION OVEN

Cooking with a convection oven can seem more complex at first but is easy to master with some simple tips. With convection cooking, you'll be cooking fast and delicious meals in no time. Here are a few basic steps to get started.

STEP 1: DETERMINE IF RECIPE CONVERSIONS ARE NEEDED

Check your recipe to see if you need to adjust the time and/or temperature for your convection oven. Some recipes provide times and temperatures for both conventional and convection ovens. Your product manual will let you know exactly how you should adjust. The Auto Convect Conversion feature, which is available on select Maytag convection ovens, helps you convert your traditional recipes to the correct convection time and temperature with ease.

STEP 2: CONVERT RECIPE TEMPERATURE

If you need to adjust the recipe temperature, simply subtract 25°F from the temperature listed.2 For example, if the temperature listed is 375°F, adjust to 350°F.

STEP 3: CONVERT RECIPE TIME

For True convection ovens that help speed up cooking when roasting meats1, multiply the listed time by .80.2 For example, if the time listed is 60 minutes, adjust to 48 minutes.

STEP 4: PREHEAT OVEN

Preheat your oven to the correct converted temperature. Select Maytag ovens come with special features like Power Preheat to help you start cooking sooner.

STEP 5: START COOKING

Set your timer for the converted time and place your dishes on the oven racks for consistent heat and even cooking.

Why Should You Use the Convection Setting?

1. It cooks faster: Because hot air is blowing directly onto food instead of just surrounding it,

food cooks about 25 percent faster in a convection oven.

2. It cooks more evenly: Regular ovens can have hot spots, depending on where the heating element is, but the fan in a convection oven will circulate the air to help even out the temperature variances.

3. It's better at browning: Air in a regular oven can become a bit humid, as moisture can't escape. Convection creates a dry atmosphere that caramelizes the sugars faster when roasting, so foods like meats and vegetables get browner, but the interiors stay moist.

4. It saves energy: Because food cooks faster in a convection oven, and generally at a lower

temperature, it's a bit more energy efficient than a regular oven.

When Should You Use the Convection Setting?

Because there are so many benefits to convection, you're probably wondering why most convection ovens still have a regular oven setting. Depending on what you're making, there are instances when you actually don't want a fan circulating hot air around.

When to Use the Convection Setting

- Any time you're roasting: Foods that are roasted, like meats and vegetables, really benefit from convection cooking. They cook faster, more evenly, and the drier environment yields crispy skin and caramelizes exteriors much better.

• When baking pies and pastries: Convection heat melts fat and creates steam faster, which helps create more lift in pie doughs and pastries like croissants.

• When making lots of cookies: Convection allows you to bake more than one tray of cookies at a time evenly without the need to rotate them partway through baking.

• Any time you're making something that's cooked with a cover: If you're covering up the food with a lid, like a braise, or covering a casserole dish with foil, moisture loss is not an issue, so you might as well cook on convection since it'll cook faster.

- When you're toasting or dehydrating: When you toast or dehydrate food, the goal is to remove moisture as quickly as possible, so convection is more efficient than regular.

When Not to Use the Convection Setting

The fan becomes a liability around delicate foods that start out as batter and set while cooking. Blowing air on these foods can create lopsided results. Don't use convection when making these foods:

- Custards and flans

- Souffles

- Cakes

- Quickbreads

- Breads: While some argue that convection creates even browning and a great crust, others say that it dries out the interior of the bread. The choice here is really up to you.

How to Use the Convection Setting

If you've decided to use the convection setting, here are a few things to keep in mind:

- Lower the temperature: Lower the recommended oven temperature by 25°F.

- Check earlier: Because food cooks more quickly on convection, check on it two-thirds or three-quarters of the way through the recommended cooking time and make any necessary adjustments.

• Make sure air can circulate: Convection is only effective if the air can circulate well over the food. Use trays, roasting pans, and baking pans with lower sides, and don't cover the oven shelves with foil.

Don't be afraid of your convection oven — embrace this great feature! Play around with it and you'll probably be amazed by the results.

What not to bake in a convection oven

Not everything is compatible with a convection oven's fan. Delicate baked goods, like souffles, custards, angel food cake and even many quick breads aren't suitable for convection. The air flow can cause cakes to rise unevenly, the tops of cupcakes to lean towards one side and dry out the top of custard, creating a crust that you don't want.

Use convection for roasting meat and vegetables, baking cookies and pies, and anytime you want even browning.

5 Tips for Baking with the Convection Setting

Once upon a time, convection ovens were the coveted white whale for home cooks with a passion for baking — always talked about in hushed, reverent tones and rarely seen outside professional kitchens. These days, every newly renovated kitchen seems to have one, but having one doesn't automatically mean we know how to use them.

First of all, understand that "convection" is a setting on your oven, not the oven itself, and it's usually controlled by a switch or a button near the other controls. When it's on, you are baking with convection heat; when it's off, it's just a regular oven and bakes as usual.

What happens when that convection setting is on? Your oven heats as usual, but a fan and exhaust system are engaged. These respectively blow and pull hot air through the oven and around your food. This means that the air directly around your food maintains a very steady temperature, helping your food cook more quickly and evenly. The exhaust system also pulls moisture out of the oven, so food becomes more crisp and brown.

Convection ovens can be either gas or electric, so when not using the convection setting, you'll experience all the advantages and disadvantages of cooking in those respective ovens.

1. Lower the temperature by 25°F.

Because heating and cooking is so efficient in a convection oven, you usually don't need quite as high a temperature to get the same results. A good rule of thumb is to set the oven to about 25°F below the recommended temperature of your recipe.

2. Check food frequently toward the end of cooking.

Also thanks to all this efficiency, your foods will usually cook a little more quickly than usual. Check on your food halfway through the recommended cooking time to gauge how quickly cooking seems to be coming along, and then check more frequently near the end of cooking. Go by how your food looks and smells to tell when it's done, rather than by the timer. As you get used to baking with the convection setting, you'll get a better feel for how quickly certain things cook and can feel more confident predicting the timing.

3. Don't crowd the oven.

Because convection relies on air being able to circulate, be careful of overcrowding the oven and blocking the flow of air. The food will still cook, but the cooking will be less efficient and you'll lose the advantage of the convection setting. It's fine to bake on multiple racks, but try not to fill the racks wall-to-wall.

4. Use low-sided baking sheets and roasting pans.

The convection setting also works best if you use low-sided pans or rimless baking sheets, especially when baking cookies or roasting vegetables. This allows for better air circulation around the food and helps crispy foods become even crisper. (Although note that this is less important for things like casseroles and cakes, which rely on the high sides of their pans to hold their shape and where crisping isn't as important.)

5. Don't use convection for cooking cakes, quick breads, custards, or soufflés.

While these dishes would benefit from the steady heat, the movement of the air from the fan and exhaust system can cause them to cook unevenly or to rise less impressively. Custards can also form an unpleasant crust on the surface as they dry out in the wicking action of the oven.

Buying a convection oven

There are many types of convection ovens on the market. The most common is a conventional oven with a built-in fan, allowing you to turn the convection setting on and off.

The best ones have an additional heating element by the fan, which makes the air moving around the oven a consistent temperature. A consistent temperature means the oven will cook more evenly than models with just a fan. To find ones with the extra heating element, look for terms like "third-element convection," "true convection" or "European convection" when you're shopping around.

If you want a gas range with a convection oven, look for dual-fuel options. Gas ovens don't offer convection options without the ability to switch over to electric.

Also, the bigger, the better. Bigger insides allow the air to circulate more freely. This is why full-size ovens cook more evenly than smaller countertop versions.

The Convection Oven and Its Types

An oven plays a big role when it comes to cooking, whether it is for baking, stove-top cooking, broiling steaks, or roasting a turkey or chicken, the oven can do it all.

Ovens usually have a prized place and are a must-have appliance in every kitchen. The reason for this is the oven's multiple functions and versatile operations.

Furthermore, when it comes to ovens, the preferred type is the convection oven—this is not a surprise because using a convection oven has several benefits which a conventional oven does not normally offer. Because of the edge the convection oven has over a regular range, it usually costs more than a regular oven.

Types of convection ovens

There are several types of convection ovens, but the most common types are divided into 2 categories. The first type is differentiated by the placement of the fan and additional heating element; this is the regular and the true convection oven.

The second type is classified by its placement or position in the kitchen; the major types are the countertop convection ovens and the floor models.

Classified by fan placement

Regular convection oven

A regular convection oven is a regular oven that has an additional fan found at the back of the oven to help in the circulation of the air within the oven's interior.

In this type of convection oven, the fan blows both hot and cold air to and fro within the oven.

As a result of the variance in the air being blown, the food may not be as evenly cooked as expected.

True convection oven

A true convection oven, on the other hand, is an oven which has a fan as well as a third heating element that is found at the back of the oven. The true convection oven is often referred to as the European convection oven.

Unlike the regular convection oven that circulates pre-heated air, the true convection oven distributes heated air by its fan. Therefore, the result is evenly cooked food.

Classified by convection oven placement

Countertop convection oven

Countertop convection ovens can be placed on counters, tables or any open space. Countertop convection ovens often come portable, smaller, and lighter, and are perfect for small areas or spaces.

When it comes to food, this type can only accommodate small and limited amount. One edge of this type of convection oven is its easy installation and removal.

Floor model convection oven

A floor model convection oven is significantly bigger and can accommodate cooking more food at one time than a countertop convection oven. It comes in half and full size, depending on the space available.

A floor model convection oven is the preferred type for restaurants and other food establishments for it allows simultaneous cooking of large volumes of food at a faster pace.

CONVECTION OVEN RECIPES

The following recipes are convection oven-friendly while also being a treat to the taste buds. Try some of these convection oven recipes today.

Maple Balsamic Roasted Vegetables

Prepartion time

1 hour 10 minutes

Ingredients

- 1 1/2 pounds whole thin rainbow carrots

- 1 1/2 pounds sweet potatoes peeled chopped into 1 inch cubes

- 2 small red onions cut into thick chunks

- 1/2 pound rutabagas peeled and diced

- 1 1/2 pounds parsnips peeled and sliced thinly

- 1/3 cup olive oil

- 2 tsp sea salt

- 2 tsp black pepper

- 1 tsp fresh chopped rosemary

- 1 1/2 tbsp dry herb de provence

- 1 cup maple syrup

- 1/4 cup balsamic vinegar

Instructions

1. Preheat the oven to 350 degrees F.

2. In a large bowl combine all of the vegetables. Add the oil, salt, pepper, herbs and rosemary and toss to coat well.

3. Place the vegetables on a large roasting pan or two baking sheets, making sure they are all level and not on top of one another.

4. Place in the oven and cook for about 45 minutes, checking that the point of a sharp knife spears the vegetables easily.

5. When the vegetables are cooking in the oven, place the maple syrup and balsamic vinegar in a pan and bring to a boil.

6. Reduce the heat and simmer slowly until it has reduced by about half and is nice and thick.

7. Once the vegetables are ready, lightly drizzle some of the syrup over them and return to the oven for 5 more minutes.

8. Serve warm or store in the refrigerator until ready to use.

HOMEMADE ROTISSERIE CHICKEN

Prepartion time

9 hours

Ingredients

Chicken rotisserie marinade

- 4+ pound Whole chicken

- .5 bottle lemon juice

- .25 cup white wine

- .25 cup extra virgin olive oil

Chicken rotisserie rub

- 1 tablespoon Honey

- 3 tbsp unsalted butter

- 1/4 cup brown sugar

- 4 tsp garlic powder

- 1/2 teaspoon dried oregano

- 1/4 teaspoon dried thyme

- 1/4 teaspoon dried basil

- Kosher salt and freshly ground black pepper

instructions

Marinade

1. Clean cavity of whole chicken, wash and pat dry.

2. Combine all marinade ingredients and mix.

3. Pour into a large freezer bag and add the whole chicken.

4. Refrigerate for 4-6 hours.

Rub

1. Remove chicken from the marinade.

2. Melt the butter and honey in the microwave and mix.

3. Evenly brush the butter and honey mixture on and inside the chicken.

4. Mix all of the dry ingredients and apply it to the entire chicken.

5. Tuck wings underneath chicken and truss the legs together with twine.

6. Run rotisserie rod through the cavity of chicken and insert the rotisserie forks into the skin of the chicken.

7. At 350 degrees F, a whole chicken takes about 20 to 30 minutes per pound to cook.

8. Therefore, a 4-pound chicken should take 1:20 – 2 hours to cook.

9. Use a meat thermometer to test the internal temperature. When chicken reaches 175 to 180 degree F, it is done.

Huevos Rancheros Bake

Prepartion time

1 hour 45 minutes

Ingredients

- 1 lb bulk chorizo sausage

- 1 red bell pepper, chopped

- 1 cup chopped onions

- 1 can (28 oz) Muir Glen™ organic fire roasted crushed tomatoes, undrained

- 1 can (4.5 oz) Old El Paso™ chopped green chiles

- 1 package (1 oz) Old El Paso™ original taco seasoning mix

- 1 can (15 oz) Progresso™ black beans, drained, rinsed

- 2 cups shredded Mexican cheese blend (8 oz)

- 8 eggs

- ½ cup milk

- ½ teaspoon salt

- ½ cup diced avocado

- ½ cup crushed Food Should Taste Good™ blue corn tortilla chips

- 2 tablespoons chopped fresh cilantro leaves

- Lime wedges

Instructions

1. Heat oven to 350°F. Spray 13×9-inch (3-quart) baking dish with cooking spray.

2. In 12-inch nonstick skillet, cook sausage, bell pepper and onions over medium-high heat 7 to 8 minutes, stirring occasionally, until sausage is no longer pink; drain, and return mixture to skillet.

3. Reduce heat to medium; stir in tomatoes, green chiles and taco seasoning mix.

4. Heat to simmering.

5. Cook 4 to 6 minutes, stirring frequently, until liquid thickens.

6. Remove from heat.

7. Stir in black beans and 1 cup of the cheese; transfer to baking dish.

8. In medium bowl, beat eggs, milk and salt with whisk until blended.

9. Stir in remaining 1 cup of cheese.

10. Pour evenly over sausage mixture in baking dish.

11. Bake uncovered 40 to 45 minutes or until eggs are set and knife inserted in center comes out clean.

12. Cool 5 minutes.

13. Top with avocado, chips and cilantro. Serve with lime wedges.

Sheet Pan Chicken Pot Pie Recipe

Prepartion time

1 hour 15 minutes

Ingredients

- 2 Tablespoons butter

- 4 celery stalks (diced)

- 4 carrots, (sliced)

- 1 onion (diced)

- 2 red potatoes (diced)

- 2 teaspoons minced garlic

- salt and pepper, to taste

- 1/4 cup flour

- 2 cups chicken broth

- 1 (8 ounce) package cream cheese

- 2 cups rotisserie chicken (shredded)

- 1/2 cup frozen peas

- 1 (17.3 ounce) package Pepperidge Farm Puff Pastry Sheet (thawed)

- 1 egg

- 2 Tablespoons fresh parsley (finely minced)

Instructions

1. Preheat oven to 400 degrees F.

2. Melt butter in a large saucepan over medium-high heat.

3. Add celery, carrots, onion and potatoes.

4. Saute for 8-10 minutes, or until vegetables begin to soften.

5. Add garlic and season with salt and pepper.

6. Mix in flour, chicken broth and cream cheese.

7. Let cook for 5 more minutes, stirring constantly.

8. Fold in chicken and peas.

9. Pour mixture into a baking sheet sprayed with nonstick cooking spray.

10. Roll out two puff pastry sheets to the width of the sheet pan, cut into 1-inch strips and lay over filling.

11. Use a sharp knife to cut off any excess dough hanging over the sides.

12. Whisk egg in a small bowl and brush over the top of the pot pie.

13. Cook for 30-35 minutes, or until the top is golden brown.

14. Remove from oven, garnish with fresh parsley and serve.

Fresh Homemade Peach Pie

Prepartion time

3 hours 40 minutes

Ingredients

- Pastry for a 9-inch single-crust pie

- 1 package (8 oz.) cream cheese, at room temperature

- 1 1/4 cups sugar

- 6 1/2 cups sliced peeled firm-ripe peaches (about 4 lb.)

- 3/4 cup orange juice

- 1/4 cup cornstarch

- 1/4 cup lemon juice

Instructions

1. With a fork, prick bottom and sides of unbaked pastry in pan at about 1-inch intervals.

2. Bake in a 375° regular or convection oven until golden, 15 to 20 minutes; let cool on a rack.

3. Meanwhile, in a bowl, mix cream cheese and 1/2 cup sugar until smooth.

4. Spread evenly over bottom of cool pastry.

5. In a blender or food processor, whirl 1 cup sliced peaches, remaining 3/4 cup sugar, orange juice, and cornstarch until smooth.

6. Pour into a 3- to 4-quart pan; stir over medium-high heat until mixture boils and thickens, about 4 minutes.

7. Remove from heat and stir in lemon juice.

8. Add remaining 5 1/2 cups peaches to hot peach glaze and mix to coat slices.

9. Let cool until tepid, about 25 minutes, then scrape onto cream cheese mixture in crust.

10. Chill, uncovered, until firm enough to cut, at least 3 hours.

11. Cut into wedges and serve, or invert a large bowl over pie (it shouldn't touch fruit) and chill up to 1 day.

Convection Oven Sweet Potato Fries Recipes

Prepartion time

40 minutes

Ingredients

- 2 large sweet potatoes, peeled and cut into matchsticks

- 2 tablespoons olive oil (or melted coconut oil)

- 1 teaspoon kosher salt

- 1/2 teaspoon garlic powder

- 1/2 teaspoon cayenne (or paprika)

- ½ teaspoon black pepper

Instructions

1. Heat the convection oven to 375ºF. Line a baking sheet with parchment paper or foil.

2. In a large bowl, toss the cut sweet potatoes in oil. Once fully coated, toss with ½ teaspoon salt, the garlic powder, cayenne, and black pepper.

3. Spread the sweet potatoes onto the baking sheet without overcrowding. Bake for 15 minutes, then use a spatula to flip the fries and rotate the pan. Continue to bake for 10 to 15 minutes, until crisp.

4. Remove the pan from the oven and sprinkle the remaining ½ teaspoon of salt over top. Use the spatula to toss the fries in the salt once more. Serve hot.

Lemon Square

Prepartion time

35 minutes

Ingredients

- 1 stick of butter

- 1 cup sugar

- ¼ cup powdered sugar

- 1 teaspoon of grated lemon peel

- 2 eggs

- 1-1/4 cups of flour

- 3 tablespoons of lemon juice

- 1 teaspoon of baking powder

Instructions

1. Mix together the powdered sugar and butter until light and fluffy. Gradually add 1 cup of flour until it is mixed well. Place the mixture into a

shallow casserole baking dish. Bake dish for 10 minutes at 350°F.

2. In a medium bowl, mix together the left over flour and baking powder, adding in the eggs one at a time. Beat mixture slowly and gradually add the remaining ingredients. Pour mixture over the crust.

3. Bake dish at 350°F for 15 minutes. Let bars cool completely before cutting them into squares.

Brown Sugar and Garlic Chicken

Prepartion time

40 minutes

Ingredients

- 10 cloves of garlic minced

- 1/4 cup of olive oil

- 1/4 cup to 1/2 cup of brown sugar

- 8 boneless, skinless chicken breasts

- Pinch of salt and pepper

Instructions

1. Sauté the minced garlic on the stovetop until it turns golden brown.

2. Gradually add the brown sugar until it forms a thick consistency and remove from heat.

3. Season the chicken with salt and pepper and place in a baking dish and pour mixture evenly over chicken.

4. Cook at 500°F degrees for 30 minutes.

Sweet Potato Fries

Prepartion time

40 minutes

Ingredients

- 2 large sweet potatoes, peeled

- 1 1/2 tablespoons olive oil

- 1/2 teaspoon salt

- 1/2 teaspoon ground cinnamon

- 1/4 teaspoon ground ginger

Instructions

1. Peel the sweet potatoes then slice them into ¼ inch long slices and ¼ inch wide. In a bowl mix together the oil, salt, cinnamon and ground ginger.

2. Gradually add the sliced potatoes to the bowl until all of them are coated evenly.

3. Place the potato slices on the high rack and bake at 350°F for 15-20 minutes.

4. Bake for a few minutes longer if you enjoy your fries extra crispy.

Pepper Steak

Prepartion time

15 minutes

Ingredients

- 4 steaks (preferably New York Strip or T-Bone)

- ¼ teaspoon of dry basil

- 2 tablespoon ground pepper

- ¼ teaspoon of garlic salt

Instructions

1. Evenly sprinkle and massage pepper onto both sides of steak.

2. Next, sprinkle the garlic salt and basil over both sides.

3. Place steak on the high rack. Grill at 400°F for 10 minutes.

Tuna Noodle Casserole

Prepartion time

25 minutes

Ingredients

- 1 (3 ounce) can of tuna, drained

- 1(2 ounce)can of cream of mushroom soup

- 6 ounces of egg noodles, cooked

- 1/2 cup peas

- 1/2 cup sour cream

- 1 cup cheddar cheese shredded

- 1/4 cup bread crumbs

Instructions

1. Cook egg noodles to al dente.

2. In a bowl mix together the tuna, mushroom soup, sour cream and peas.

3. Once mixed together add in the cooked egg noodles.

4. Place mixture into a 10-inch casserole dish.

5. Spread the bread crumbs and cheese over the top of the casserole evenly.

6. Place dish on the high rack and bake at 375°F for 15-18 minutes. If the casserole topping becomes too brown, cover with aluminum foil.

Dijon Herb Chicken Breasts

Prepartion time

50 minutes

Ingredients

- 4 chicken breasts, bone in, skin on (can also replace with drumsticks)

- 2 tablespoons Dijon mustard

- 1 tablespoon olive oil

- 1/2 yellow onion, sliced

- 1/2 cup low sodium chicken stock

- 4 sprigs parsley leaves, chopped

- 2 teaspoons garlic, chopped

- 1 teaspoon sugar

- 1 teaspoon red chili flakes

- 2 teaspoons salt

- 1 teaspoon black pepper

Instructions

1. In a large bowl mix together all ingredients besides the chicken and onion.

2. Once all ingredients are evenly combined add in the chicken and onion.

3. Place plastic wrap over top of bowl and let chicken marinade for at least 45 minutes.

4. Once chicken is ready to cook place on the high rack, skin side down.

5. Cook the chicken at 350°F for 7-10 minutes per side.

6. Once cooked allow chicken to sit 3-5 minutes before eating.

Holiday Spiced Nuts

Prepartion time

15 minutes

Ingredients

• 4 cups nuts (pecans, walnuts, cashews and/or almonds)

• 6 tablespoons butter melted

• 4 teaspoons Old Bay seasoning

• 1/2 teaspoon cayenne pepper

• 1 teaspoon sea salt

Instructions

1. In a medium bowl, mix together the seasonings with the melted butter.

2. Place nuts in a separate bowl and gradually add the butter seasoning mix until they are coated evenly.

3. Place coated nuts in a shallow baking dish.

4. Cook the nuts at 350°F for 7-10 minutes.

5. Once cooked, carefully place nuts onto parchment paper to cool.

Parmesan Scallops

Prepartion time

15 minutes

Ingredients

- 16 sea scallops with muscle removed

- 4 tablespoons butter

- 4 teaspoons lime juice

- 3/4 cup of grated parmesan cheese

Instructions

1. Wash and remove the muscle on the side of the scallops.

2. Gently pat dry and place in a shallow baking dish.

3. Place a dollop of butter on top of the scallops.

4. Next evenly distribute lime juice over all the scallops.

5. Sprinkle the parmesan cheese over all the scallops and bake at 350°F for 7-10 minutes.

Honey Lime Chicken Breasts

Prepartion time

45 minutes

Ingredients

- 4 boneless, skinless chicken breasts

- 1/2 cup honey

- 1/3 cup soy sauce

- 1/4 cup lime juice

Instructions

1. Combine the honey, soy sauce and lime juice in a gallon sized zip lock bag.

2. Add the chicken to the bag and let marinate for at least 30 minutes in the refrigerator.

3. Once chicken has marinated place the breasts on the high rack and dispose of the leftover marinade.

4. Cook for 8-10 minutes per side at on for at 350°F.

5. Depending on the thickness of the chicken (these times are based on the 1-inch thick chicken breasts).

6. Let the chicken rest for 5 minutes before serving.

Roast Turkey

Prepartion time

35 minutes

Ingredients

- 1 (12-14-pound) turkey

- 1/4 cup olive oil

- 1 tablespoon paprika

- 1 teaspoon black pepper

- 1 teaspoon salt

- 2 stalks celery, chopped

- 2 medium onions, chopped

- 2 large carrots, chopped

Instructions

1. Combine all the spices together and rub the turkey with them and olive oil.

2. Mix together all the vegetables and then stuff turkey with them.

3. Add the extender ring to the glass bowl.

4. Place turkey on the low rack, breast side down.

5. Roast the turkey at 350°F for 13-15 minutes per pound.

6. Be sure to let the turkey sit for at least 10-15 minutes before serving.

CHOCOLATE CREAM CHEESE

FROSTING

Prepartion time

45 minutes

Ingredients

- 3 c all-purpose flour

- 2 c sugar, white

- 1/3 c baking cocoa

- 2 tsp baking soda

- 1 tsp salt

- 2 c water

- 3/4 c vegetable oil or coconut oil (updated from original)

- 2 tsp vanilla extract, I use pure and a tad less on measure

- 2 tsp vinegar

CHOCOLATE CREAM CHEESE FROSTING

- 1 pkg cream cheese, softened (8 oz)

- 1/4 c butter, you can use margarine in a pinch but use butter!

- 2 c confectioners' sugar

- 1/3 c bakers cocoa

- salt

- 3 Tbsp milk

- 1/2 tsp vanilla extract

Instructions

1. In a mixing bowl combine the dry ingredients (The first five.)

2. Add the water, oil, vanilla, and vinegar.

3. Mix well (batter will be thin).

4. Pour into a greased 13x9x2 inch pan or 2 9-inch round cake pans. Bake at 350 for 25 to 30 minutes. Cool completely.

5. Once the cake has cooled make the frosting. For frosting, in a mixing bowl mix cream cheese, butter, and powdered sugar together until creamy.

6. Add cocoa, salt, vanilla, and milk. Mix until creamy. Then frost your cooled cake and enjoy!

Convection Oven Granola

Prepartion time

45 minutes

INGREDIENTS

- 1 1/2 cups rolled oats

- 1/2 cup slivered almonds and whole if you like

- 1/2 cup pecans

- 1/4 cup walnuts optional -- just use 1/4 cup extra oats if you don't have walnuts

- 2 teaspoons of toasted wheat germ if you have it

- 3/8 teaspoon salt

- 1 egg white medium, lightly beaten with a fork

- 3 scant tablespoons light brown sugar

- 2 tablespoons maple syrup

- 1 tablespoon honey

- 2 tablespoons oil walnut oil, coconut oil, any kind you want

- 1/2 teaspoon vanilla

INSTRUCTIONS

1. Preheat the convection oven to 275 degrees F.

2. Line a heavy, large rimmed cookie sheet with parchment paper.

3. In a large bowl, stir together the rolled oats, almonds, pecans, walnuts and wheat germ.

4. Toss in salt and stir to evenly disperse salt.

5. Pour the egg white over the oat mixture and stir well.

6. In a microwave-safe measuring cup, stir together the brown sugar, maple syrup, honey and oil.

7. Heat on high for about 1 minute, then stir to dissolve sugar slightly.

8. Stir in vanilla. Pour hot syrup mixture over granola and stir until evenly coated.

9. Dump oat mixture out onto the two cookie sheets, spreading as evenly as possible and pressing down slightly so that oats are in a thin, closely packed layer

10. Bake for 35 to 45 minutes in the convection oven stopping to stir every 15 minutes. The granola should be nicely browned, but still kind of soft when you take it out of the oven. It should crisp up as it cools.

Homemade pizza in a convection oven

Prepartion time

1 hour 45 minutes

Ingredients

To make the pizza base

- ¾ tsp Yeast

- ½ tsp Sugar

- ⅓ cup Water

- 1¼ cups Flour

- Salt to taste

- 1 tsp Onion Powder (optional)

- 1 tsp Butter

- Olive oil to grease

Topping

- Green capsicum

- Baby corn

- Tomatoes

- Onion

- Carrots

- Optional

- Coriander and garlic butter to brush on the crust

- Oregano

Instructions

To make the Pizza base

1. Heat the water for 15 to 20 seconds in the microwave or if you are using some other method to heat the water make sure the water is warm to touch and not extremely hot and if you

have a food thermometer the water should be between 120°C to 125°C.

2. To feed the yeast add sugar and stir it.

3. Next, add they east and let it sit. We are using instant dry yeast hence we don't need to stir the yeast granule as they easily dissolve in the warm water.

4. Now leave the yeast mixture for 10 minutes.

5. Once there is a foamy layer on the top of the water your yeast is activated.

6. Now add the foamy yeast mixture to the dry ingredients and knead the dough for 10 minutes.

7. Add the butter and knead for an additional 5 minutes. I know you need to work with the dough to get that perfect bread.

8. Grease the bowl with olive oil and cover the whole dough with olive oil too.

9. Let the dough rest for anywhere between 45 minutes to an hour. (Preferably keep the dough in the same place where the yeast was kept to proof)

10. To know that your dough is ready to need to check if it is doubled in size or else keep it in a warmer place for an additional 15 minutes.

11. Once your dough is proofed (doubled in size), your dough is ready. Now punch down the dough and form a circular base.

12. Now place the dough down in the pan of your choice. And with a knife or a fork puncher down the pizza base so that it doesn't rise.

To top your Pizza

1. Add some sauce to the pizza base.

2. Next, add some mozzarella cheese and the toppings of your choice. I have added some processed cheese also because I like the saltiness of it.

3. Now brush some coriander garlic butter on the crust and add some oregano. I add some oregano before baking the pizza as I like the cheese and herbs to combine.

4. Now comes the part of convection baking. As in a convection oven, the heat comes directly from the top rods. So, I would recommend you to set the temperature to 170°C and bake your pizza for 20 minutes as there is no direct heat

from the bottom. Slow cooking the pizza would bake the pizza properly.

5. And if you are anything like me and you like bubbly brown cheese. Then keep the pizza for 2 to 3 additional minutes on 200℃. Keep an eye on it.

Toaster Oven Chocolate Cookies

Prepartion time

27 minutes

Ingredients

- 1 1/2 tablespoons Unsalted Butter, softened

- 3 tablespoons Brown Sugar (see note)

- 1 large egg yolk, reserve white for another use

- 1/4 teaspoon Vanilla Extract

- 2 tablespoons Unsweetened Baking Cocoa, (not Dutch-processed)

- 1/4 cup White Whole Wheat Flour (see note)

- 1/4 teaspoon Baking Soda

- Pinch Fine Sea Salt

- 3 tablespoons Chocolate Chips, divided

Instructions

1. In a medium bowl cream the butter and sugar with a hand-held mixer until light and fluffy (about 2 minutes).

2. Mix in the egg yolk and vanilla.

3. Place the mixer on the lowest speed and add cocoa powder, flour, baking soda, and salt. Mix just until combined. Stir in 2 tablespoons of the chocolate chips.

4. Chill cookie dough in the fridge for at least 10 minutes.

5. While the dough chills preheat your toaster oven to 350°F. Lightly oil your cookie sheet or line with a silicone baking mat.

6. Roll chilled dough into tablespoon-sized balls. Place at least 2 inches apart on the prepared pan. Gently press the remaining chocolate chips into the top of the dough.

7. Bake until the cookies are set but the centers are still puffed and soft, 5 to 7 minutes. The cookies will continue to bake as they cool.

8. Allow cookies to cool for a few minutes on the pan before transferring to a cooling rack.

Apple Crisp

Prepartion time

55 minutes

Ingredients

- 5 ½ cups sliced baking apples

- 1 ½ teaspoons fresh lemon juice

- ¼ teaspoon grated lemon zest

- ¼ cup granulated sugar

- ½ teaspoon ground cinnamon

- ¼ teaspoon salt

- ½ cup rolled oats

- 2/3 cup packed brown sugar

- 1/3 cup flour

- ¼ teaspoon baking powder

- ½ cup (1 stick) margarine (or butter)

Instructions

1. Preheat oven to 350 degrees on convection setting, 375 degrees in a conventional oven.

2. Place apples in a large bowl and sprinkle with lemon juice and zest. In a small bowl, combine

sugar, cinnamon and salt. Sprinkle over apples. Stir lightly to moisten sugar mixture and arrange apples in an 11-by-7-inch or 9-by-9-inch baking pan.

3. In a medium bowl, combine oats, brown sugar, flour and baking powder. Add margarine in pieces and work in with two forks or pastry blender to form a crumbly mixture. Sprinkle evenly over apples in pan.

4. Bake in preheated convection oven 40 minutes (45 minutes conventional) or until top is bubbling and lightly browned.

5. Serve warm or cold with ice cream or whipped cream, if desired.

Chocolate Nut Brownies

Prepartion time

40 minutes

INGREDIENTS:

- 1/2 cup unsalted butter

- 2 ounces unsweetened chocolate

- 1 cup sugar

- 2 eggs

- 1 teaspoon vanilla

- 2/3 cup all-purpose, unbleached flour

- 1/2 cup chopped nuts (I used walnuts)

- 1/2 teaspoon baking powder (Decrease to 1/4 teaspoon for high altitude)

- 1/4 teaspoon salt

Instructions

1. Heat oven to 350 degrees. Grease (with butter) and lightly flour bottom only of 8 or 9-inch square pan.

2. In a large saucepan, melt butter and chocolate over low heat, stirring constantly.

3. Remove from heat; cool slightly.

4. Blend in sugar.

5. Beat in eggs, one at a time.

6. Stir in remaining ingredients.

7. Spread in prepared pan.

8. Bake at 350 degrees for 25 to 30 minutes or until set in center. * Be sure not to overbake if you want a softer center.

9. Remove from oven and cool completely on a wire rack.

10. Cut into bars to serve.

Best Chocolate Chip Cookie Recipe

Prepartion time

1 hour 5 minutes

Ingredients

- 2 cups all purpose flour

- 3/4 cup ground oats

- 1 1/2 teaspoon baking soda

- 1 teaspoon salt

- 3/4 cup unsalted butter melted

- 3/4 cup brown sugar

- 3/4 cup sugar

- 1 teaspoon vanilla extract

- 2 large eggs

- 12 ounce semi-sweet chocolate chips

- 1 cup English toffee bits

Instructions

1. Place a heaping 3/4 cup of dry oats in the food processor.

2. Process until finely ground.

3. Dump both sugars and the vanilla extract in the bowl of an electric mixer.

4. Turn on low and add the melted butter, mix to combine. With the mixer running, pour in the eggs.

5. Add the baking soda, salt, and slowly add the flour and powdered oatmeal.

6. Scrap the bowl and mix to combine, then fold in the chocolate chips and toffee bits.

7. Chill the dough for at least 30 minutes, OR form into a log on a piece of freezer paper.

8. Wrap and freeze.

9. Preheat the oven to 325 degrees F (300 degrees F convection.)

10. Line baking sheets with parchment paper and place equal two 2 1/2-tablespoon portions on the baking sheets 3 inches apart.

11. Use either a cookie scoop or cut the frozen dough into rounds.

12. Bake until the edges are golden, but the centers look slightly under baked.

13. Remove from the oven and cool on the cookie sheets until firm enough to pick up. (Baking time varies greatly on the temperature of the dough and whether you are baking with a conventional oven or convection. Conventional: chilled dough 15-20 minutes, frozen dough 20-

25 minutes. Convection: chilled dough 10-12 minutes, frozen dough 18-22 minutes.)

Toaster Oven Baked Pears Recipe

Prepartion time

40 minutes

Ingredients

- 1 Red Anjou Pear, (ripe)

- 1/8 teaspoon Ground Cinnamon

- 6 Semisweet Chocolate Chips

- 2 tablespoons Chopped Pecans

- 1 teaspoon Pure Maple Syrup

Optional Toppings:

- Plain Greek Yogurt

- Vanilla Ice Cream

- Whipped Cream

Instructions

1. Adjust toaster oven cooking rack to the bottom position and preheat to 350 degrees F. Lightly oil a baking dish or cookie sheet.

2. Halve pear and use a teaspoon to scoop out the seeds. If the halves do not lay flat, slice a thin piece off the back.

3. Place pear halves in the baking dish and sprinkle with cinnamon, fill with chocolate chips and pecan pieces.

4. Drizzle maple syrup over both halves.

5. Bake until pears soften about 25 to 35 minutes.

6. The bake time will vary depending on the variety and ripeness of the pear used.

7. Serve warm topped with vanilla ice cream or yogurt.

Creme Brulee

Prepartion time

50 minutes

Ingredients

- 6 egg yolks

- 3 cups sugar

- 32 ounces cream

- 1 vanilla bean

- Turbinado sugar for sprinkling on top

Instructions

1. Heat cream over medium heat until warm.

2. Mix eggs and sugar together with cream, beat together until white paste.

3. Slowly temper in the cream, making sure not to scramble eggs.

4. Pour into 4- to 6-ounce ramekins, set inside water bath in oven, bake on 325 degrees for 45 minutes.

5. Once done and cooled, sprinkle with Turbinado sugar (sugar in the raw), and use blow torch.

Eggless apple cake recipe

Prepartion time

50 minutes

INGREDIENTS

- 1 cup - 240ml

- Apple - 2

- Wheat flour / atta - 1 cup

- All purpose flour / Maida - 1 cup

- Powdered sugar - 1 cup

- Baking powder - 2 tsp

- Baking soda - 1/2 tsp

- Cinnamon powder - 1/2 tsp

- Vanilla essence - 1/2 tsp

- Milk - 1 cup

- Melted butter - 1/2 cup + 1 tbsp (150 gms)

- Cooking oil - 1 tbsp

- Water - 1/2 cup (to grind apple)

Instructions

1. Wash and chop apple into small cubes. Grind to a puree adding water.

2. In a wide bowl sieve wheat flour, maida, baking powder, baking soda and cinnamon powder.

3. In another bowl mix melted butter, milk, vanilla essence and apple puree.

4. Add the sieved dry flours and mix without lumps. Lastly add 1 tbsp cooking oil and mix well.

5. Transfer the apple cake batter to a greased baking pan. Bake in a preheated convection oven for 40 minutes. Check with a tooth pick and remove the cake after warm.

6. For microwave apple cake, take 1/2 cup of cake batter in a microwave safe glass bowl.

7. Cook for 4 minutes. Remove it by checking with a tooth pick. Enjoy when warm.

8. Apple cake stays good only for 2 days. So try to consume it quickly.

Chocolate Babka

Prepartion time

1 hour 30 minutes

Ingredients

Syrup:

- 1/2 cup sugar

Dough :

- 3/4 cup whole milk

- 10 grams (One-and-a-half 1/4-ounce packets) active dry yeast

- 2 1/2 cups bread flour, sifted, plus more for dusting the work surface

- 2 1/2 cups pastry flour, sifted

- 2 large eggs

- 1/2 cup plus 1 tablespoon sugar

- 1/2 teaspoon pure vanilla extract

- 1 teaspoon kosher salt

- 1 stick (8 tablespoons) unsalted butter, at room temperature

- 30 ounces chocolate hazelnut spread, such as Nutella

- 1 cup semisweet chocolate chips

Instructions

For the syrup:

1. Put the sugar and 2/3 cup water in a small saucepan over medium-high heat and bring to a boil.

2. Reduce the heat and simmer until the sugar dissolves, about 2 minutes. Remove from the heat and let cool.

3. Cooled syrup can be refrigerated in an air-tight container up to 1 month.

For the dough:

• Combine the two flours and the dry yeast.

• Put the milk in the bowl of an electric mixer fitted with the dough hook or in a large bowl.

- Add in order, the combined flours and yeast, eggs, sugar, vanilla, salt and 4 tablespoons of the butter.

- Mix on low speed or with your hands until all the ingredients are combined and the mixture is sticky, 3 to 4 minutes.

- Increase the speed if using a mixer, and slowly add the remaining 4 tablespoons butter in small chunks and mix until the dough is elastic, a bit shiny and very smooth, about 4 minutes.

- Put the dough on a work surface lightly dusted with flour and knead by hand until it starts to feel inflexible, about 2 minutes.

- Shape the dough into a square.

- Transfer to a baking sheet, cover tightly with plastic wrap and refrigerate until the dough increases in volume by about 30-percent, 8 to 12 hours.

For the babka:

1. Transfer the chilled dough to a work surface lightly dusted with flour.

2. Use a rolling pin to roll the dough into a 1/5-inch-thick rectangle about 10-by-28-inches.

3. Spread the chocolate hazelnut spread evenly over the dough, then sprinkle with the chocolate chips.

4. Roll the dough tightly like a jelly roll and lay seam-side down.

5. Use a serrated knife to cut the roll into thirds, then cut each third in half lengthwise.

6. Using two dough pieces, lay one across the middle of the other so they form an "X." Twist each end once or twice, so the babka resembles a simple braid.

7. Repeat with the remaining dough pieces so that you have three babka loaves in all.

8. Transfer each babka to an 8-by-4-inch loaf pan, and tuck the ends under.

9. Cover each pan with a dry towel and let rise until the loaves double in volume, about 1 hour. (For best results, place a bowl of warm water at the bottom of an oven that hasn't been turned on, then place the loaves inside the oven and shut the door.)

10. Preheat a convection oven to 350 degrees F. (Alternatively, preheat a conventional oven to 350 degrees F.)

11. Bake the loaves until cooked through and the tops are crisp and golden brown, about 25 minutes in a convection oven.

12. If the tops start to turn dark brown and are still not cooked through, cover with parchment or foil to prevent burning. (Cook about 30 minutes in a conventional oven.)

13. Remove the babkas from the oven and immediately brush them with a generous amount of syrup.

14. Let cool before removing from the pans.

Old Fashioned Rice Pudding

Prepartion time

3 hours 15 minutes

Ingredients

- 1 cup arborio rice

- 1 tablespoon vegan butter

- 7 cups almondmilk, unsweetened, sounds crazy but it is really 7 cups, you can also use sweetened almondmilk and leave out the coconut sugar

- 1/4 cup coconut sugar, if you use sweetened almondmilk leave out this coconut sugar

- 1/3 teaspoon ground cinnamon

- 1/3 teaspoon ground nutmeg

- 1 cup raisins

- 1 teaspoon vanilla extract

Instructions

1. Preheat the oven to 325 degrees.

2. Lightly butter a 9" x 13" glass baking dish.

3. Next pour in the almond milk, rice, raisins, all the spices and the vanilla.

4. Mix it in the dish. I use my fingers and spread the rice over the bottom as evenly as I can.

5. Dot the vegan butter over the top.

6. Put it in the preheated oven and bake for 2-½ to 3 hours.

7. Check it at 2 to 2-½ hours and see if it is the creamy moisture that you like. See if the rice is done. You may bake it longer if you think it is still too wet.

8. At the end of baking there will be a baked 'crust' on the top of the casserole. You just remix it all in the casserole and serve warm or cold.